1
Museum

Written by Sarah Elsworth
Illustrated by Stephen Axelsen

Contents

Harcourt Achieve

Rigby • Saxon • Steck-Vaughn

www.HarcourtAchieve.com
1.800.531.5015

The Bones Museum

With these characters . . .

Charlotte

Mrs. Bird

Bert

"He stuck his paw throug[

Setting the scene . . .

When Charlotte has to visit her favorite
museum with Mrs. Bird, she takes her
little cat Bert along, hidden
in her jacket.

Just as Charlotte notices the "No pets"
sign, Bert escapes into the exhibits.

Mrs. Bird talks nonstop in a booming
voice. Bert keeps popping up among the
exhibits. It's a museum visit Charlotte
will remember . . .

he dinosaur's eye . . ."

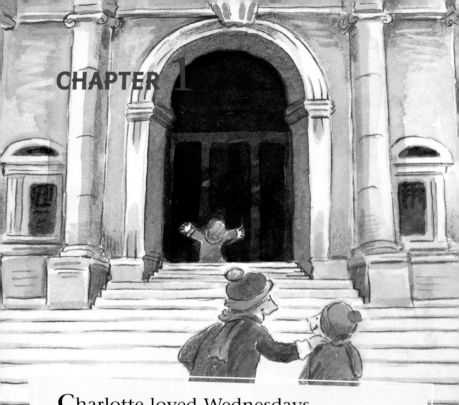

CHAPTER 1

Charlotte loved Wednesdays.
Wednesdays were a half day at her
school. Every second Wednesday she
and her mother visited the Museum of
Natural History. Charlotte called it
"The Bones Museum" because it had
lots of different types of skeletons
and bones to look at—dinosaur bones,
bird bones, and crocodile bones. There
was even a huge skeleton of a whale.

Charlotte's mom was a doctor at Central Hospital. She had every second Wednesday off. But one Wednesday she said she couldn't make it to the museum.

"I'm sorry, sweetie," Charlotte's mom said. "I have to work this afternoon. But I've arranged for Mrs. Bird from next door to take you. You remember, she's a paleontologist, an expert on fossils. It'll be a really special visit!

Charlotte's heart sank. Mrs. Bird had a big booming voice and she snorted when she laughed. She *did* know a lot about dinosaurs, though. Charlotte tried to sound positive.

"Sure Mom, that'll be nice," she said.

As Charlotte was getting ready, she had an idea. If her mom couldn't go with her, she would take Bert, her little cat.

Bert was no ordinary cat. He was more like a person. He slept at the end of Charlotte's bed, and Charlotte told him everything. Bert always listened very attentively, and he never licked himself or looked bored when she was talking to him.

9

Charlotte had often told Bert about the museum, and she was sure he would love to see the bones. When Mrs. Bird rang the front doorbell, Charlotte slipped Bert inside her jacket. His whiskers tickled her neck, but he did feel nice and warm, a bit like a hot water bottle.

"Hello there, Charlotte!" bellowed Mrs. Bird. "Are you ready for a lesson in paleontology?"

Oh boy, thought Charlotte. *It's going to be an interesting day . . .*

Mrs. Bird talked to Charlotte as they walked to the museum. "Did you know that paleontology is not just the study of dinosaurs, Charlotte?" she asked. "It's the study of all ancient living things."

Charlotte found it hard to answer, because Bert was wriggling so much inside her jacket. A couple of times he tried to pop his head out. Luckily Mrs. Bird didn't seem to notice.

No
food
or drink.
No flash
photography
No pets

TICKETS

12

When they got to the museum, Charlotte and Mrs. Bird joined the line for tickets. Charlotte didn't see the big sign just near the ticket booth that said "No food or drink. No flash photography. No pets."

By now Bert was getting very hot and cross and he was starting to meow. Charlotte had to cough so he wouldn't be heard. When she coughed for the third time, Mrs. Bird turned around.

"Charlotte, that sounds like a nasty cough. You'd better tell your mother."

When she turned back, Charlotte
loosened her jacket a bit so Bert had a
little more space. Suddenly, Bert burst
out of her jacket and made a flying leap
toward a toddler in a passing stroller.

"Kitty! Kitty!" screamed the little
girl in the stroller. She bounced up
and down excitedly and said, "Meow,
Meow."

Bert got a fright and streaked off in
the direction of the dinosaur exhibit.

The mother pushing the stroller stopped and spoke to the little girl. "Aren't you clever, darling? You made sounds like a kitty. But there's no kitty here—not in a museum." The little girl continued with her shrieks of "Kitty! Kitty!"

At that moment Charlotte saw the sign saying "No pets." *Oh, no,* she thought. This meant trouble. She must find Bert as quickly as possible.

"Come on now, Charlotte" said Mrs. Bird. "Our turn is next." They bought their tickets and made their way into the museum.

CHAPTER 3

When Charlotte saw the dinosaur exhibit, she felt a little shiver of excitement. This was her favorite part of the museum.

As they approached the first dinosaur, Mrs. Bird motioned for Charlotte to stop.

"Although dinosaurs as we think of them are now extinct, there is a form of dinosaur still alive today. Do you know what that animal is, Charlotte?" she bellowed. Her voice echoed in the hall.

Hmm, I should know this, thought Charlotte. She was puzzling over the answer when something caught her eye. A fluffy white tail was making its way up the dinosaur's head. Bert! How could Charlotte get him down from there?

Just then Mrs. Bird's voice interrupted her thoughts. "Mmm? Charlotte? Do you know what that animal is?"

"Um . . . No, I don't, Mrs. Bird," she said.

"Well, then I'll tell you, dear. It's the bird. Yes, birds are descended from dinosaurs. They share characteristics that some dinosaurs had: feathers, a wishbone, and a three-toed foot."

As Charlotte listened and nodded she could see Bert peering at her through the dinosaur's eyes.

That cheeky cat! Charlotte tried hard not to laugh. He stuck his paw through the dinosaur's eye and waggled it about. Oh, what if Bert damaged the exhibit! She would be in *big* trouble.

21

22

Happily, Mrs. Bird didn't seem to notice that Charlotte was distracted.

"Now, this is an Ankylosaur; he's a very special dinosaur because . . . "

Charlotte listened, her eye on Bert all the time. Now he was creeping down the dinosaur's spine. Then he leapt onto the floor. Charlotte moved closer. She hoped she could scoop him up and put him straight back into her jacket.

Suddenly, a school group appeared. By the time they had passed, Bert was nowhere to be seen. What on earth was she going to do now? As she racked her brain she could hear Mrs. Bird's voice resounding down the hall.

"Hurry along, Charlotte. There's much more to see . . . "

CHAPTER 4

By now Charlotte was worried. What if she couldn't find Bert before it was time to go home?

She followed Mrs. Bird into the African mammals exhibit. "Charlotte, these exhibits are fascinating. They so accurately depict . . . " Charlotte only heard fragments of Mrs. Bird's commentary. "Habitat is . . . mandrill . . . markings . . . "

Charlotte stared at the elephant of the savannah. He seemed to have a strange furry growth in the crook of his trunk.

Bert was asleep in the elephant's trunk!

Mrs. Bird was busy reading the museum map.

Charlotte went closer. "Bert," she whispered. "Come here!"

   Bert opened his eyes and yawned.
When he saw Charlotte he jumped
down and started rubbing his back
against the model tree.

   Charlotte gestured sternly to him
to come out. But Bert was enjoying
himself. He strolled around to the front
of the elephant and started to use its
leg as a scratching post!

"Oh, no," murmured Charlotte. "I can't believe he's doing this."

Just then Mrs. Bird called out, "Charlotte! Let's have a break, dear. I'm desperate for a cup of coffee."

Charlotte glared at Bert as she followed Mrs. Bird to the cafe.

CHAPTER 5

At the cafe, Charlotte lined up with her tray. She ordered drinks and muffins for them both. As Charlotte was waiting for her milk she heard a rustling noise behind the coffee machine. She looked up and saw Bert's flicking tail among the stacks of paper cups.

"Bert," she growled. "Come here this instant."

Bert leaped to the floor, knocking over the towers of paper cups as he went. Cups rained down on Charlotte and rolled away under the counter.

"Oh, dear," Charlotte said to the boy at the cash register, who looked a bit puzzled. "I'm sorry. I don't know how I knocked those cups over."

She paid for their snacks and joined Mrs. Bird. Luckily Mrs. Bird hadn't noticed the mess at the cash register.

While Mrs. Bird summed up the highlights of the day, Charlotte smiled. She'd just had a brainstorm. She tipped a little milk on her saucer and slipped it under the table. A minute later she heard a 'clink' as Bert took a drink of milk.

Pretending to pull up her socks, Charlotte bent down and slipped a tired Bert inside her jacket. "Now be good and stay there," she whispered.

"What did you say, Charlotte?" said Mrs. Bird.

"Just what a lovely time I've had, Mrs. Bird," Charlotte replied.

"I'm so glad you enjoyed your trip with Mrs. Bird," said Charlotte's mother that night.

"It was more exciting than I expected," said Charlotte.

"I'm sorry I missed it. Good night then, you two. Look at you, Bert! Fast asleep already and you've done nothing all day."

Charlotte's mother turned off the light. She didn't see Charlotte and Bert smiling in the dark.

"Bones and Skeletons"

" Old bones and huge skeletons.
  Let's go to see them,
  Dearest Bert", said Charlotte,
    "They're at the museum."

But Bert escaped into the museum
Oh Charlotte, he's naughty!
  Let's hope you soon see him.
" No Bert! Come down from the
    dinosaur's spine!
Eek! Come here pur. . . lease,
    there isn't much time."
Some milk on a plate will work
    every time.